I0440637

LIPP FAMILY HISTORY

Germany to America

By

Katherine Fletcher

2015 Copyright Katherine Fletcher All Rights Reserved

ORIGIN OF THE LIPP FAMILY

The Lipp family comes from a region called Westphalia, Germany. This is in between the Rhine and Wesser Rivers. Surnames were used in this region after the 12th century and often referred to locality.

The name could come from a short form of Phillips, such as Phillipp von Hessen who was known as LIPS. The name could also come from "LIPPE", the name of a place in Westphalia. This means the first LIPPE named ancestor could have lived there and moved to another city.

Other spellings of the LIPP name include Lippe, Lipps, Liipsius, Lipple and others. The name is closely identified in early medieval times. Lippe was one of the smallest states in Germany until around 1945. There is also a river Lippe that runs through Westphalia. There is a man named Arnold Lipper or von der Lippe in 1222. This family would evolve as a noble family with lots of involvement in history.

INTRODUCTION

This book covers the Lipp family from Germany and their migration to America in the late 1700's. They came from Germany to escape poverty and religious prosecution. They also liked the idea of owning their own land. They settled in Virginia mostly with some lines going to Maryland, Illinois, Texas, California and Ohio.

You'll love the story of how a mother and daughter tricked the Confederates during the Civil War.   Also the men who joined the California Gold Rush in the 1860's.   There are many interesting stories about the Lipp family and their contributions to American history.

GENERATION ONE

Harriet Olivia Lipp 1908-1998

GENERATION TWO

Carvallis Mendiceno "Bud" Lipp (1856-1943) and Harriet Amanda "Hattie" Thompson (1858-1933)

> Birth 11 Nov 1856 in Fredericksburg, Culpepper Co., Virginia USA
> Death 23 Jan 1943 in Clinton, Prince George's Co., Maryland USA

This man was a tinner by trade.

> Harriet Amanda Thompson was Birth 22 Feb 1858 in Jonesboro, Greene Co., Tennessee USA
>
> Death 22 Sep 1933 in Washington, DC USA

Here is her obituary:

Funeral services for Mrs. Harriet T. Lipp, 75, prominent worker in the Hamline Methodist Episcopal Church, who died Friday at her home, 1520 Buchanan street northwest, will be held at 2 p.m., tomorrow from the Hamline church at Sixteenth and Allison streets northwest. Burial will be in Rock Creek Cemetery. Officers of the church will act as pallbearers.

"Mrs. Lipp had lived in Washington since 1879. She was president for 10 years of the Women's Foreign Missionary Society, and taught a Bible class named after herself. She is survived by her husband, Carvallis M. Lipp, and four children."

The Washington Post, 24 Sep, 1933, page 2. ProQuest Historical Newspapers.

Harriet's parents are Sylvanus H Thompson and Sarah Elizabeth Lane. They were from Greene County, Tennessee.   Here's a picture of Harriet's mother, Sarah Lane who made such an impressive contribution to the Civil War.

Here's is her picture – Sarah Elizabeth Lane

Harriet Thompson picture

This photo was taken in the backyard of her home, which was the end row house at 1520 Buchanan St., NW, Washington, DC. She used to prepare the communion elements at her home and walk down the alley to Hamline Methodist Church.

THIS IS AN AMAZING STORY OF THE CIVIL WAR and HARRIET AND HER MOTHER'S PART IN IT

GIRL WHO SAW CONFEDERATE GENERAL TAKEN GIVES STORY

Mrs. C. M. Lipp on Porch of Tennessee Home When John Hunt Morgan Was Captured.

The capture and arrest of Gen. John Hunt Morgan of the Confederate army was personally witnessed by Mrs. C. M. Lipp of 1520 Buchanan street, who, as a small girl, stood on the veranda of her home in Greenville, Tenn., while her mother, Mrs. Sarah Thompson, serving as a dispatch carrier for the Union army, revealed to Gen. Sherman and his officers the hiding place of the famous Confederate leader.

Mrs. Lipp's father, Capt. Sylvanus Thompson, although a native of Tennness, was a Northern sympathizer, and it was at the sacrifice of many of his friends and the love of many relatives that he openly sided with the Northern Army, eventually being shot while on reconnaissance duty in their service, leaving behind him two little daughters and his wife, who continued to carry on his work with the Union side.

"Well do I remember the day that my father was shot," recalled Mrs. Lipp. "My mother was sent for by some neighbors and, taking me with her, we went to a barn outside of our town where they had lain my father's body. He had been shot through the head. It was after that that my mother sent word to Gen. Sherman that she would disclose to him the whereabouts of Gen. Morgan. Gen. Sherman with his army entered Greenville, and I can remember clinging to my mother's skirts as she directed the men to tear down the fence of a neighboring house. There they found Gen. Morgan hiding behind some vines.

"Mother was obliged to leave Greenville after that, so when Sherman retreated he took my mother, my little sister and myself with his army, placing us in one of the canvas-covered transport wagons of the army. We later transferred to a train which took us to Canton, Ohio, and there my mother became a nurse in one of the Northern hospitals, keeping us with her during that time."

Mrs. Lipp relates that her mother carried many important dispatches on horseback for leaders of the Union Army. "She had lovely, long hair," said Mrs. Lipp, "and frequently she would braid the dispatches in her hair. Once she told us that she was captured while carrying an important message and she was obliged to swallow the paper in order to prevent its being found."

Carvallis Mendiceno Shipp
(age unknown)

CELEBRATE THEIR GOLDEN WEDDING

Mr. and Mrs. C. M. Lipp, 521 Randolph street, who celebrated the fiftieth anniversary of their wedding last night, at their residence, when they received their friends from 8 to 10:30 o'clock. Mr. and Mrs. Lipp have been residents of Washington since 1879, having been active members of the Hamline Methodist Episcopal Church for over 40 years. They were married 50 years ago in Chattanooga, Tenn. Mr. Lipp, a member of the Board of Trade and Masonic orders, is in the sheet metal business.

photo:

Carvallis Mendiceno Lipp, daughter-in-law Evelyn Reeves Lipp, and nurse. Clinton, Maryland. 1942

Here's a newspaper posting about a fall from a roof.

"Tinner Lipp Falls from a Roof." **Carvallis M. Lipp**, of 301 H street northeast, is at the Emergency Hospital, suffering from the effects of a fall from the roof of a house near the corner of Ninth and K streets. He was engaged in reroofing the house, and stepping too near the edge, fell into a pile of wreckage below. The injured man was taken to the Emergency Hospital, where it was found that he had a fractured arm and a bad cut on the forehead. His wife called at the hospital shortly after he had been received there. **Mr. Lipp** is a dealer in stoves and tinware at 1529 Seventh street northwest." **Source:** *The Washington Post*, 4 Oct 1896

ANOTHER STORY I FOUND WAS ABOUT A TRIP TO CHATTANOOGA, TN TO HONOR WILLIAM H. LIPP

My dad, Carl C. Lipp, Jr., told me that he remembers going with his grandfather, C.M. Lipp, and his cousin, Charles Morris, to the 1925 faithful service dinner at which W.H. Lipp was honored. Charles drove C.M.'s new Chevy. There was no trunk, so the luggage was piled in the back seat next to my dad. The weather was hot, the windows were down. My dad had to keep an eye on his grandfather who was chewing tobacco and, every so often, would have to spit out the window. Dad had to roll up his window in a hurry. On the return trip, they stopped at Lockout Mountain in Tennessee and there is a photograph of C.M. sitting on a large boulder, feet dangling over the side.

ANOTHER STORY ABOUT THE TINNER AND PROHIBITION

My Dad (Carl C. Lipp, Jr.) told me that during the prohibition years, C.M. Lipp used his sheet metal skills to make a still which he operated at his business. The vent pipe went up along the wall of the next building and high enough that the fumes couldn't be smelled by police officers walking along the street. He put the alcohol in half gallon glass jugs inside of metal kerosene containers that he had fitted with a false bottom. The kerosene could still pour out from the top in case of search. His wife, Hattie, was opposed to drinking and never knew about the still.

Dad also told me that his grandfather drank at his shop and hid the bottle in the back room in a bin of fittings. One day a worker was welding, when a spark flew into a box of oakum and flamed up. While everyone ran for water, CM ran to save his bottle that was hidden nearby in the bin.

ANOTHER GREAT STORY ABOUT CARVALLIS BY HIS GRANDSON CARL C. LIPP

"My grandfather (*C.M. Lipp)* was skilled at his craft and took pride in his work. He was a sheet metal worker. This true happening took place in Chattanooga, Tenn. Just over 100 years ago.

" When my Grandfather was a young man he worked with his older brother doing sheet metal work. In those days, a sheet metal worker would design, and create by hand, the fancy metal cornices that were used on buildings. Putting a new metal roof on a house, chicken house or barn was also a part of their craft. My story concerns another phase of their business: installing, repairing and working on Hot Air Furnaces whether in a house or barn. Tobacco growers had taken a liking to these large cast iron furnaces to speed up the tobacco drying process. The furnaces were often called an Octopus because of the many round heat pipes that radiated out from the top of the monster. The furnace was usually located in the center of the barn to make it easy to run the many heat pipes over a wide area of the barn. This central location of the furnace had one drawback, it made it necessary to run the sizeable smoke pipe horizontally across the barn before you could go thru a wall and then have the usual vertical pipe, extending above the barn roof, which gives a draft to the fire.

"It was a pleasant Sunday morning, and as my Grandfather and his young wife were leaving church, they stopped to chat with one of my Grandfather's customers, a tobacco grower. The tobacco grower said he had a major problem and needed some help real soon. He had a barn full of tobacco and the furnace wouldn't work. My grandfather said, as soon as they had their Sunday supper he would come out for a look. True to his word, he arrived at the tobacco barn in midafternoon and it didn't take long for him to diagnose the problem. Someone had been burning green wood in the furnace without the proper draft and the entire 60 feet of 12 inch horizontal smoke pipe was blocked solid with soot. The tobacco grower agreed it would be satisfactory if my Grandfather came out in the morning to take care of the problem.

" Monday morning was another beautiful day and my Grandfather looked forward to the trip to the country, but not to the very dirty job he would have as soon as he got there. From past experience he knew that when he was finished, he would be black from head to toe with only two white circles for his eyes. As he was leaving the shop on the wagon he got a bright idea. It wasn't really his idea. He had heard a couple of fellows talk about an easy way to clean out smoke pipes that were stopped up and he thought this was an ideal time to give it a try. A quick stop at the hardware store and he was on his way again. Arriving at the barn he confidently unloaded his small purchase and walked directly to the furnace. He opened the furnace door, placed the two pound container of black powder in the furnace, lit the short fuse, closed the furnace door and hurried outside to see if it worked. A muffled whoomph was followed by a great big swish. Every bit of the soot had been blown out of the pipe. The job had been quickly and successfully completed—or had it??? Suddenly, a bright sunlit morning turned to midnight. A huge cloud of soot had obliterated the sun. To make matters worse, the breeze was carrying the cloud toward the city. AND – Monday is wash day.

" I was very pleased that my Grandfather had seen fit to tell me of this experience in his life. I never was able to learn if this was the reason that my Grandfather and his bride left Chattanooga the following year, and moved to Washington, where he opened his own sheet metal shop under the name of **C. M. Lipp**. It was some years later, when my grandfather saw fit to take my father in as a partner, that the name was changed to **C. M. Lipp & Son**. The name remained the same until my father died. At that time we added the Inc. My Grandfather and father have passed away. I have retired, and my son and my wife are carrying on the business on the same block where it started in 1886."

Source: story written by **Carl C. Lipp, Jr. about 1975**

HERE'S CARVALLIS DEATH CERTIFICATE INFORMATION

Carvallis M. Lipp, died Jan 23, 1943, at 10:45 p.m., age 86 yrs, 2 mos, 12 days, of Cardiovascular and renal disease in Clinton on Route 5, Prince George's County, Maryland. He was born Nov. 11, 1856 in Fredericksburg, Virginia, to **Henry Wm. Lipp** (born in Virginia) and **Frances E. Huffman** (born in Virginia). He was widowed and his wife's name was **Harriet T. Lipp**. His son, **Carl C. Lipp** of 3159 Tennyson st., NW, provided the information. Funeral director, The S. H. Hines Co., 2901 14th St., NW. Burial at Rock Creek Cemetery, Washington, DC **Source:** Maryland State Department of Health, Certificate of Death 851, Reg. Dist. No. 235

Their children:

Harriet Olivia 1908-1998 married Howard Fenton Phillips Jr.

Clarence M. Lipp 1877-1890 died at age 13 of pulmonary issues in Washington DC

Ada Fern 1880-1969 / married Herman Lavely Cochran and Joseph Arthur Rose

Ora Frances 1881-1974   married Cyrus Morris / died in Jackson, Missouri

Herbert Thompson 1883-1908

THE SUICIDE OF HERBERT – AGE 24

"KILLS HIMSELF WITH ACIDDespondent Tinner Makes Death Sure by Using Razor on Wrist " **Herbert T. Lipp**, a tinner, twenty-five years old, 1524 Fourteenth Street, northwest, committed suicide at 11 o'clock yesterday morning in the basement of the house at the above address. He

drank a quantity of carbolic acid, and slashed his left wrist with a razor. Coroner Nevitt issued a certificate of death from suicide. The remains were turned over to an undertaker. " **Lipp** had been married but a short time, and had lived in Fourteenth street for a number of years with relatives. He was employed in a shop near Fourteenth street and Park road, and until this week had been attentive to his duties. Persons living in the house noticed that the man had become despondent, and tried to comfort him. It was thought that he had been worrying over financial troubles. " Yesterday morning **Lipp** left home as usual for his work. He stopped at a drug store on his way, his friends say, and purchased a bottle of carbolic acid. Returning to the house about 10 o'clock, he went to his room and procured a razor. He again left the house, but after descending the front steps turned into the basement. He stayed there for some little time, and a relative, who had gone to that part of the house, discovered him lying on the floor. His wrist was cut, and blood flowed freely from the wound. He had drunk some of the acid. " A doctor was summoned, and **Lipp** was taken to his own room. He was suffering greatly. Restoratives were used, and for a time is was thought that the man would live. He was in great agony. He lived but two hours after being taken from the basement of the house. He is survived by a widow."
Source: *The Washington Post*, Washington, DC,

February 7, 1908 " **MR. LIPP** TAKES LIFE. Drinks Carbolic Acid, After Cutting Arteries in Wrist. " After endeavoring to end his life by severing the arteries in his wrist, **Herbert T. Lipp**, twenty-four years old, a tinner living at 1415 Park road northwest, drank a quantity of carbolic acid at the home of his father 1524 Fourteenth street northwest, yesterday morning, about 11 o'clock, and died a few minutes later. " A coil of rope, which he had evidently intended using should his other attempts prove unsuccessful, was found at his side. No motive for the suicide has been learned. Members of the family refused to make a statement last night. " **Lipp** was discovered by his mother, who heard his groans. She summoned her husband, **C. M. Lipp**. Entering the basement, **Mr. Lipp** found his son lying unconscious on the floor. Beside him lay a tumbler which had contained the acid, and a coil of stout rope, which he had evidently contemplated using. " The father summoned Dr. J. A. Flynn, of 1323 Q street northwest. Coroner Nevitt was notified and issued a certificate of death by suicide." Source: *The Washington Herald*, February 7, 1908, Page 2.

Paul Henry 1887-1951 / married Edith Sloan and Jamie Wood / lived in California

Carvallis Christy "Carl" Lipp 1894-1958 married Evelyn Adah Reeves

GENERATION THREE

Henry William Lipp (1814-1860) and Frances Jane Huffman (1822-1892)

> Birth 28 Sep 1814 in Madison County, Virginia, USA
> Death 28 Jan 1860 in Atlanta, Fulton Co., Georgia

He married Frances Jane Huffman in 1840 at age 25. He is a miller by occupation.

> Frances Jane Huffman Birth 12 Oct 1822 in Fredericksburg, Culpeper, Virginia, USA

> Death 22 Feb 1892 in Chattanooga, Hamilton Co., Tennessee USA

Frances married Henry Lipp in 1840. After his death in 1860 she married Frederick Devine in 1871 and moved from Virginia to Chattanooga, TN.

France's parents are James Huffman and Mary Hurt Finks. Her grandparents are Samuel and Eve Huffman from Madison County, Virginia.

STORY ABOUT DEATH AND SICKNESS OF HENRY LIPP

Henry W. Lipp was sick with a lung problem. He and his family were moving south to a warmer climate for his health. They got as far as Atlanta when he became too ill to travel further and he died not long afterwards. Late in the summer of 1864, General Sherman captured Atlanta and ordered all non-military people to leave, with the choice of going north or south. The family probably left at that time. From 22 June 1982 letter from Betty Donaldson

THeir Children:

Clarance Lipp

Sarah Ellen "Sallie" lipp 1842-1911 married James Reeves Allison

Mary F. Lipp 1844-1878 married Henry Hamel and P.A. Wilkinson. Died at age 34 in Chattanooga, TN of yellow fever.

James T. 1847-1877

William Henry 1849-1942 married Elizabeth J. Bush

Palmyra C. "Polly" 1853-1900 married John Evans

Carvallis Mendiceno "Bud" 1856-1943 married Harriet Thompson

GENERATION FOUR

Thomas Lipp (1791-1870) and Sarah "Sally" Huffman (1792-1878)

> Birth 12 Sep 1791 in Culpeper Co., Virginia USA
> Death 20 Apr 1870 in Putnam Co., Missouri USA

He married in Madison County, VA and in the 1850 census shows up in Ralls, Missouri as a farmer.

He died Putnam County, Missouri in 1870 at age 78.

Sarah Huffman

Birth 2 May 1792 in Madison Co., Virginia USA Death 16 May 1878 in Putnam Co., Missouri USA

Her parents are Benjamin Huffman and Caroline Lipp.   Her grandparents are Jacob Huffman and Barbara Souther from Madison County, VA.

THOMAS AND SARAH'S CHILDREN ARE:

Eleanor Frances 1813-1891 married John Shaver

Their children:

Henry William 1814-1860 married Frances Huffman

Wesley Powell   1822-1896 married Minna Tiele and also went to California and Peru for mining.   He was one of the first gold miners in El Dorado in 1850.

Martha Ann 1822-1871 married Joshua Franklin Snider

Here's her picture

Caroline M. 1827-1899 married Joseph Richardson Biggers

Lucinda France 1829-

Thomas F 1830-1898 married Elizabeth Jane Peck / went thru sickness, bad crops and started over. Here's an interesting biography of Thomas F.   from ancestry and the Monroe County History.

> Commencing in the affairs of life a young man without a dollar, he went to work with energy and resolution to succeed, and his industry has not been unfruitful of substantial results. But

misfortunes fell upon him, sickness, bad crops, etc., and twice his hard-earned accumulations were swept away, leaving him to begin again at the foot of the ladder. Since 1874 he has steadily advanced toward the front as a substantial farmer of the township. Since then he has paid for his farm - from the first $80, which he had paid in cash on purchasing it. This is an excellent place of 280 acres worth over $8,000, and besides this he has fully stocked his farm with cattle, horses, hogs, etc. Having succeeded in getting a good start sooner by far than is common, now that he has obtained it he will doubtless go forward in situating himself comfortably in life with more than ordinary celerity. As everyone knows the first $1,000 is harder to make than the next $10,000. Mr. Lipp is a native of Virginia, born in Madison county on the 13th day of September, 1830. His parents, Thomas Sr., and Sarah (Hoffman) Lipp, removed to Missouri when he was six years of age, and located in Ralls county, where they resided 10 years. They afterwards made one or two other removals, and finally settled permanently in Putman county, where the father died in 1871. Thomas Jr., was reared partly in Ralls county, and up to the age of 21 had had but a four months term at school. He afterwards attended school another four months term, and on the 23d of March 1854, was married to Miss Elizabeth J., a daughter of Elijah and Elizabeth J. (Harrison) Peck, formerly of Kentucky. He then rented a farm and engaged in farming, with little or nothing to go upon but his own muscle and energy, for he had only one horse to plow with. In a couple of years he had saved from his earnings $500, but moving to Florida Mills, sickness fell upon his family, and this was all spent besides $100 of indebtedness he was compelled to incur. After the health of his family was restored he engaged again in farming, this time in Ralls county, and in a few years he had gathered about him considerable stock and had gotten a respectable start, but the Federal soldiers came along and stripped him of his horses, etc., and the hog cholera destroyed all his hogs, a fine drove of 100 head, so that he was left with nothing on earth but his wife and children, their household effects and a milch cow, the soldiers having taken all his other stock except his hogs, which the cholera made way with. The following winter he spent making rails for money to buy bread and meat with for the family, and he walked five miles to and from his work. That was a pretty blue time with him, but his courage and resolution never for a moment faltered. The next spring he went to farming again, and the wonder naturally arises how he managed to farm without anything to farm with or on. Where there is a will there is a way. There is a God in Israel as well as good men and kind neighbors in North America. He rented land on shares, some neighbors loaned him some unbroken young steers and a three-year-old filly. He and his family lived on corn bread and buttermilk; he broke the steers and filly, and with them raised a fine crop. He then bought his present farm on credit, paying $80 down on the purchase. But the next year the drought and chinch-bugs were extremely bad, and crops were therefore generally a failure. Soon, however, good seasons returned, the chinch-bugs disappeared, and from that time on to the present his career has been one of unbroken prosperity. He has fully paid for his farm, is entirely out of debt, and has his place well improved. Mr. and Mrs. Lipp are blessed with five children: Andrew J., Adolphus L., Elijah M., John L. and Elizabeth J. He and wife are both church members, he of the Methodist and she of the Baptist Church. He is also a worthy member of the Masonic order.

Albert Broadus 1834-1916 born in VA, died in Missouri / married Martha Frances Stockton.

Here's his picture: He was a Baptist preacher

James Benjamin   1839- married a Margaret and Anna E Davis. In 1867 he shows up in California as part of the Gold Rush.   He is listed as a miner and teamster.

THE GRAVE OF THOMAS LIPP

GENERATION FIVE

Jacob Lipp (1765) and Margaret Zimmerman

Born in Germany. Had religious confirmation at Hebron Church in Virginia in 1782 at age 17. He married Margaret Zimmerman in Culpeper, VA in 1787 at age 22.

Margaret was born in Virginia. Her parents are John Zimmerman (1711-1776) and Ursula Blankenbaker (1732-1832). Her father John came from Bietigheim,

Ludwigsburg, Baden-Wuerttemberg, Germany and died in Virginia.

Their Children:

Elizabeth Lipp 1789-1870 married William Mitchell

Thomas Lipp 1791-1870

Margaret Polly Lipp 1794 –

GENERATION SIX

Henrich H. Lipp (1707-1792) and Mary Elizabeth Brooks (1719-1768)

Henrich was born in Germany and died in Culpeper, VA. He came to Virginia before 1776. He lived in Madison County, VA. He came from Germany during the Revolutionary War and deserted the British Army.

Elizabeth was born in Germany and died in Madison, VA.

"Henry Lipp who emigrated from Germany during the Revolutionary War and served an apprenticeship at a baker trade and when 18 years of age engaged as cook in the British Army. After landing in this country he deserted the British Army and settled in Virginia, where he married a Miss Offenbacker and reared a family of 8 children. He emigrated to Ohio and was one of the first settlers of that state. He lived to be 89 years of age and died at the home of his daughter in Winchester, Indiana. His wife died many years before, probably about 1827."

From Lipp and related families of Clinton Co., Indiana, 1828-1983, by Francis Lamar Lipp, 1983.

Their children:

Henry 1758-1847 born Germany, died Preble, Ohio / married Eve Offenbacker/

Daniel 1760-1796 born Germany, died Virginia

Anna Maria 1762 – married Christopher Zimmerman

Caroline 1762-1835 married Benjamin Huffman

Elizabeth 1765- married Daniel Goode

** Elizabeth and Jacob are twins

Jacob 1765- married Margaret Zimmerman

Henry Lipp Jr. married Elizabeth Zerfas / moved family to Indiana

>Henry's son John was a pioneer of Clinton County, Indiana, born in Warren Co, Ohio 1818

Barbara

Rachel

Sarah

Peter

GENERATION SEVEN

John Christian Lipp (1687-1787) and Mary Elizabeth Ewald (1700)

John was born and died in Germany. Mary Elizabeth Ewald also born in Germany.

Their children were:

Henrich H. 1707-1792 married Mary Elizabeth Brooks

Henry Lipp 1720-1791

George 1721-

GENERATION EIGHT

Johann George Lipp (1667-1742) and Elizabeth (1668-1738)

> Birth 9 Oct 1667 in Fellbach, Rems-Murr-Kreis, Baden-Württemberg, Germany

> Death 16 Dec 1742 in Fellbach, Rems-Murr-Kreis, Baden-Württemberg, Germany

Married Elizabeth

Children with Elizabeth:

Anna Marie Magdalana 1685-1770
John Christian 1687-1787 married Mary Elizabeth Ewald
Johann Michael 1693-1734
Hanns Jacob 1697-

Elisabetha 1700-
Zacharias 1704-
Gottlieb 1707-

Married Anna Barbara Simaans

Children with Barbara:

Agatha 1700-
Jacob 1701-
Michael 1703-
Anna Barbara 1705-
Bernhard 1706-
Balthas 1708-1727
Johannes 1709-
Ferdinand 1711-
Johann Peter 1714-
Phillip 1720 –

GENERATION NINE

Bathasar Lipp (1630-1711) and Waldtpurga Mautz (1629-1704)

> Birth 6 Jan 1630 in Fellbach, Rems-Murr-Kreis, Baden-Wuerttemberg, Germany
> Death 22 Oct 1711 in Fellbach, Rems-Murr-Kreis, Baden-Wuerttemberg, Germany

Children with Waldtpurga :

Catharina 1655-

Johannes Goerg 1656-1727

Baby Boy 1658-1658

Magdalena 1663-

Johann George 1667-1742

GENERATION TEN

Johannes Lipp (1600-) and Catherine Scheublin (1599-1640)

> Birth 15 Jan 1600 in Ebingen, Zollernalbkreis, Baden-Wuerttemberg, Germany
> Death
>
> Catherina is Birth 1599 in Fellbach, Rems-Murr-Kreis, Baden-Württemberg, Germany
>
> Death Mar 1640 in Fellbach, Rems-Murr-Kreis, Baden-Württemberg, Germany

Their children:

Balthasar 1630-1711

GENERARTION ELEVEN

Jerg Lipp (1574-) and Anna Lipp NN

> Birth 1574 in Ebingen, Zollernalbkreis, Baden-Württemberg, Germany

Death

GENERATION TWELVE

Johann Lipp (1558)

Birth 1558 in Schietingen, Calw, Baden-Württemberg, Germany

BADEN GERMANY PHOTOS

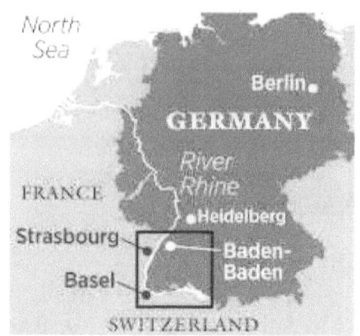

www.ingramcontent.com/pod-product-compliance
Lightning Source LLC
Chambersburg PA
CBHW050758290526
45792CB00008B/2236